Second Edition

WALKING IN LOVE

Why and How?

SUZANNE MILLER

BLUEPRINT PRESS
INTERNATIONALE

Walking In Love : Why and How?
Copyright © 2023 by Suzanne Miller

All New Testament scriptural quotations in this book are direct translations by the author from the Greek of the Nestle-Aland/United Bible Societies (NA/UBS) text - The Greek New Testament, 4th Revised Edition - published by the Deutsche Bibelgesellschaft (German Bible Society). The single quotation from the Hebrew Scriptures (Deuteronomy 5) is taken from the New International Version of the Bible (NIB).

ISBN
978-1-959365-65-5 (Paperback)
978-1-959365-66-2 (eBook)
978-1-959365-64-8 (Hardcover)

This book is dedicated to the Most Reverend Michael B. Curry, Presiding Bishop and Primate of the Episcopal Church. It was his leadership and preaching on the redemptive power of love as he picked up the torch lit by the late Dr. Martin Luther King, Jr. that, by the grace of God, motivated me to write this book.

Table of Contents

INTRODUCTION

LIVING LIFE MORE FULLY

This book addresses a goal of living life more fully in a changing world. It presents a process for accomplishing this goal that is both backward-looking (to benefit from past wisdom) and forward-looking (to address the problems of a changing world and changing circumstances). I call this process "walking in love."

Although this book is about shared humanity, it also aligns with often-neglected teachings of Jesus that pertain to achieving the goal noted above. This is no accident. I'm a lifelong Christian, so I tend to tell the story in that context. People with a different set of life experiences may tell the story a bit differently. No problem! I consider it all to be the same story told from many different points of view.

Why is this important now? I assert it is because our spiritual practices can become rigid and dogmatic and thus inadequate and unsuitable for a changing world.

What are some examples of these world changes? Birth control for those who have access to it, the explosion of the human population because of better health and improved food production, changes in our global climate, and the increase in malevolent power of individuals when you pair modern technologies for communications, weapons, and control of people with traditional fanaticism and egotism, to name a few.

Two thousand years ago or so, the world was also changing rapidly. Jesus led a spiritual revolution that broke free of old, dogmatic ideas and gave people a spirituality that was adaptable. It took the best of the old and grew it to handle the new. In this way, it actually fulfills the previous traditions.

Everything I write focuses on some aspect of human design as revealed in our common experience. I start by focusing on human inadequacy and the anxiety it provokes in us.

Spiritual people, people of faith, tend to be people of good intention. Even so, good intention only takes us so far. This is because we humans are limited in our capabilities. Those capabilities are not equal to the task of carrying out our good intentions. To be more precise, sometimes (most times?) we are not strong enough, or wise enough or caring enough.

Quite often, when those moments occur and our actions are insufficient because of our human limitations, the result is disaster— bad consequences for others. Sometimes those others are people we care very deeply about and for whom we want only the best.

This has always been a human problem, but a rapidly changing world just makes things worse.

We feel guilty and often look to shift the blame for the bad results to others.

In most cases, the "other" is God, even though we may pretend otherwise. We are angry at God for making us the imperfect creatures that we are. God has given us guidance in the form of religious teachings on how to speak and act to avoid contributing to those disasters, but our humanity limits us in putting that guidance into effect. The anger focuses on a critical question: Why create us as flawed creatures and tell us how to live, knowing that we are not capable of carrying out that guidance?

One way of handling this difficulty is to ignore it, to ignore our limitations. This is the way of the demagogue, the tyrant, the dictator, whose appeal to the community is "Give me the power and I'll fix things."

Silly person! You can't fix anything; you only make matters worse by dragging the rest of us down to failure and suffering with you after we give you the power and you misuse it in the service of your own ego! We buy into the fantasy that this time will be different, and we all pay the price.

There is an alternative: the way of love.

Consider the possibility that much of the pain and failure in the world arises because we, out of ignorance, ignore the reality of the world as it was created. Suppose the reality is that we are not designed to be independent agents, living only to ourselves.

Suppose we are designed to work together with a central power as well as each other in order to get around the ego problem. Suppose the creation is designed for us to look to the nonvisible reality within us and without us (which some call God) to complete us, to provide the wisdom, strength, and goodness that we lack.

We can do this on a one-on-one level by relating directly to the inner spiritual reality within us by asking and listening in a receptive mode for answers. We can also do this in community with others, where sharing of experience allows us to both filter out individual misunderstandings as well as pool our individually inadequate power with that of others to do more than is possible by ourselves.

I've been taught this by both my own life experience and the core of Jesus's life and teachings, as recorded in scripture. He taught this by his example as well as his words. He taught that there is such a power accessible to us. Prayer and discernment are the tools by which we access that power and align with it for the common good. It is a wonderful paradox: in furthering the common good, we also fulfill ourselves when we each carry out our own unique roles.

There is a second aspect of walking in love that is also somewhat of a paradox, given the previous discussion.

This other important aspect is also because of how humans are put together. This second aspect is brought into play as we gain more and more confidence in the goodness of God. We learn this through our own experiences and those of others in community who confide in us on these matters. In other words, after we learn to deal with the imperfect dimension of our humanity, the emphasis shifts to our perfectibility.

Jesus teaches that in one particular dimension of our humanity— loving—we are not only capable of improvement but are explicitly expected to improve. We seem to have a built-in capability to feel joy as we express love and are loved by others. We can then use the feeling of joy to lead us into becoming finished human beings in this area. We are called to become loving of others and the rest of God's creation in the same way God loves all that he has made as good.

Thus, a person who walks in love grows to depend on God to compensate for his or her inadequacies by the benefits of God's guidance and grace. Also, we are to grow in our capacity to love the same way as our heavenly Father loves.

These are the two dimensions of walking in love that this book addresses.

Chapter One

WHICH PATH?

There are three different names for the goal of living life more fully in a changing world. Why do I need to mention three different names for the same thing? Because I want to tie them into scripture, which uses all three names.

The first is *righteousness*. Righteousness is a descriptive term from scripture. It means aligning your thoughts, words, and deeds with God (the Lord), getting right with God. Walking in love is what happens to you as you take this walk. You grow more loving.

A related term from scripture is *kingdom of God*. This is the community of all who are ruled by the divine, all who live in a way governed by knowing and doing the will of God.

Throughout history, people have grappled with the problem of human limitations in wisdom and power when speaking and acting. Again and again, human beings make choices for themselves and others that turn out to be disasters. They address this need by seeking a divine source of wisdom and power to guide them and empower them.

Jesus gave his followers a new way to do this, a new path to walk that promises to finally handle this severe age-old problem of human existence.

Christian scripture tells us this in Matthew's Gospel: "Seek ye first the kingdom of God and his righteousness and every other good thing you desire will follow" (Matthew 6:33). This is the Christian perspective, but remember what was said in the introduction of this book about the primal human dilemma: "how to know and do the will of God?" This was a central issue for not only Christianity but also Judaism, as well as other religious expressions of human spirituality. The problem is the same: How can we know and do the will of the divine when we are limited in wisdom and power?

Why did the world need a new path? The old one wasn't working.

Let's start with that earlier path that Jesus, as a Jew, inherited. A central focus of it was to live out the commandments of God that were given directly to Moses by God in Sinai. Is this enough? Jesus didn't seem to think so.

This point is made very poignantly by the parable of Jesus and the rich young man, also from the Gospel of Matthew (Matthew 19:16-22). The young man approaches Jesus and says, "Teacher, what good shall I do that I might have eternal life [gain life and persist in it forever, to paraphrase the original Greek]?"

Jesus responds to him by saying, essentially, "Keep the Ten Commandments." The young man says he has kept them since his youth but asks, "What do I still lack?"

Jesus says, "If you want to be perfected, go sell what you have, give to the poor, and you will have treasure in heaven" and "Come follow me."

So two paths to righteousness are presented. The first is to follow the rules handed down by authoritative religious tradition. Let's call this rule-based religion.

The second is more. "Be perfected." Change your priorities. "Sell your goods and become my disciple." This is a departure from the traditional Judaism of Jesus's day. Instead of just following the rules, the gospel talks about becoming perfected by walking with God, under his direct rule. Let's call this connected religion.

How are the two related? How did things get this way?

There is a very telling passage from the book of Deuteronomy that puts all of this into perspective.

A central tradition I learned in Torah class was that God dictated the books of the Torah to Moses on the mountain of Sinai, and Moses wrote them down as God spoke them. This understanding is captured in Deuteronomy 5:22-27. Moses says,

> "These are the commandments the LORD proclaimed in a loud voice to your whole assembly there on the mountain from out of the fire, the cloud and the deep darkness; and he added nothing more. Then he wrote them on two stone tablets and gave them to me.

> When you heard the voice out of the darkness, while the mountain was ablaze with fire, all the leaders of your tribes and your elders came to me. And you said, "The LORD our God has shown us his glory and his majesty, and we have heard his voice from the fire. Today we have seen that a person can live even if God speaks with them. But now, why should we die? This great fire will consume us, and we will die if we hear the voice of the LORD our God any longer. For what mortal has ever heard the voice of the living God speaking out of fire, as we have, and survived? Go near and listen to all that the LORD our God says. Then tell us whatever the LORD our God tells you. We will listen and obey."

This is noteworthy. The dictated texts are considered to be the literal word of God. Note, however, that another tradition is established by this text: criticism and changing of the text is not permitted. The pious readers were free to debate the meaning of the text, but the text itself is a single, sacrosanct revelation. In other words, students of the Hebrew scriptures are taught the Torah is without blemish (i.e., contains no errors).

An alternative possibility would have been that individuals could have their own sessions with God and could then compare their experience with that of Moses. This alternative is considered and emphatically ruled out with the explanation that the Hebrew people had indeed heard the voice of God from the mountain and were afraid that hearing God in this way would result in their deaths. They explicitly made a deal with Moses, saying that God had continued to speak to him and he did not die, so they (the Hebrew people) would rely upon Moses alone to hear the direct self-revelation from God, and they would listen to it (read it) and obey.

Going back to the example of Jesus and the rich young man, the implication is that there is more to living a fulfilled life than just following the Ten Commandments. One should strive to become perfected. The religion of the people of that day was not a religion of people who, individually, heard the voice of God and passed what they heard on to the faith community. In addition, the Mosaic texts are considered to be true and unchangeable.

This story from Matthew directly lays out these two paths to achieving righteousness and its benefits. The first has people living by interpreting the meaning of the words. The words are to be taken as law, and unchangeable law at that.

The passage from Deuteronomy can be used to support an assumption that the preferred language God uses to speak to people is Hebrew. Thus, experts in Hebrew are needed to be able to explain the teachings in the context in which they were received. I know there is some truth in this because I have capabilities in several languages and am quite aware of how some things are easier to express in one language than another.

Anyway, this Deuteronomy tradition supports the idea of a perpetual corps of people whose job it is to preserve the integrity of the written revelations (scribes) as well as assist in the proper interpretation of that material (Pharisees). The Deuteronomy story implies that living rightly (righteously) by the rules will keep us aligned with God and lead to a fulfilled life.

Jesus directly challenges this assertion. This clear challenge is also recorded in Matthew's Gospel, in which Jesus says, "If your righteousness does not exceed that of the scribes and Pharisees, you will not enter the kingdom of heaven" (Matthew 5:20).

The very fact the rich young man in the gospel story is not satisfied and asks Jesus how to get more out of life corroborates this assertion. Jesus brought the idea of progress into religion. It didn't have to be once and for all but rather an evolving revelation of God as times and people change.

Note also that this is not an either-or situation. There's nothing wrong about living only by the rules, but that will not get you to a perfected state, which is a state where the dilemma regarding human limitations is effectively dealt with and the human potential for love is realized.

To my mind, Jesus teaches us how to do this. The Greek scriptures present Jesus's teachings by what they say about his life and work. This is the major difference I see between a rule-following religion and a changing, adaptable religion. Starting from a conventional Jewish background, Jesus undoes the "deal" of Deuteronomy 5 and gives each individual person the tools to learn and grow, spiritually, from direct contact with God. That is the subject of the third chapter of this book. What makes it work is the Greek concept of kenosis.

Don't misunderstand. Knowing the rules and living by them is necessary, but it is not sufficient. It's not all there is to a living religion as taught by Jesus.

There's one more point that I must emphasize that applies throughout this book: the issue of authority.

Central to the distinction between what I call connected religion and rule-based religion is the issue of authority. For the Jews of Jesus's time, this issue was clear-cut. The books of the Torah, which were said to be dictated to Moses by God on Mount Sinai, were the ultimate authority. Second in authority were the official bureaucracies charged with explaining the meaning of those scriptures.

Why is authority so important? If you believe a particular authority, such a belief relieves you of the nagging doubt associated with the question, "What if it's wrong and I take risky action in that belief that leads me to harm?"

Also, if you speak or act in a way contrary to the stated authority, the dominant culture (which does ascribe belief in that source of authority) will feel threatened and may punish or restrain you. Usually this is said to happen for the good of the people so that they are not led astray and do not come to harm.

Jesus provided an alternative way. A central element of his teaching about walking in the way of the Lord does not depend on authority external to a person's own experience. Throughout the Gospels, this point is hammered home. People challenge Jesus to cite his authority for the things he says. Instead, he speaks in ways that can be confirmed by someone testing the validity of a teaching by trying it out.

This is what I emphasize in this book. I could fill this book with tons of Bible citations, but I have resisted that urge because I want the reader to focus on the authority of personal experience and not just to read scripture. I do use stories from the Bible to point out one thing, that the teachings of Jesus that I am replicating from my own understanding and experience are still valid today, and the reader should look to his or her own experience as a primary source of authority.

The proof of the validity of what I write and what Jesus teaches in the Gospels is whether the reader's experience supports what is being said. This is at the core of walking with the Lord. You need to build up confidence through experience so that you really believe God loves you and wants only the best for you. This is trustworthy as long as a person keeps his or her eye on the risk of a particular teaching until it is tried (in a situation where "the worst that can happen" is factored in before taking the risk). Over time, this builds up confidence in the validity of the process—the confidence that God loves you and wants only the best for you.

A person does not need to walk this walk of experience by him- or herself. You can also depend on the experience of others that you see happen. I am a great benefactor of such experience. I saw another person's pain as she lived life and learned from it. I did not have to repeat her all-too-human mistakes. This was the tremendous benefit of having an older sister with whom I was close.

In the long run, the final test of experience is to look back at what has happened in your life (and the lives of others) and see the hand of God at work through hindsight. If what is being done is truly the Lord's work, you will have seen a relentless process of obstacles overcome or bypassed - nothing could stop it. The ultimate outcome is seen to have been irresistible - resistance was useless.

Chapter Two

CULTURAL CONTAMINATION

In chapter 1, I talked about two different approaches to the problem of living righteously.

One relied on a set of texts that were presumed to be true, dictated by God through particular human beings. This approach is usually accompanied by a community of people dedicated to keeping the texts error-free and interpreting their meaning. From those texts are derived rules for living that, if followed, will lead you to a life of righteousness. I called this rule-based religion.

The other approach was to have sacred texts but to allow them to be modified and supplemented based on God-given inspiration subsequent to the original definition of what constituted "sacred scripture." The acceptability of this "evolutionary religion" is based on how well it works (what the fruits of following it are). How do you know what works and what doesn't? By affirmation from the personal experiences of those who have tried the principles out in their lives and found them to be of value.

What's the difference between the two? How did these differences arise? How are we to respond to these differences?

The answers to these questions, at the core, are driven by the issue of cultural contamination.

Let me start with an interpreted assessment of why the Hebrews acted as they did in the biblical account of their encounter with God in Sinai. I'll repeat the passage from Deuteronomy 5:22-27, quoted in the previous chapter to avoid having the reader flip back and forth.

Moses is speaking to the people of Israel:

> "These are the commandments the LORD proclaimed in a loud voice to your whole assembly there on the mountain from out of the fire, the cloud and the deep darkness; and he added nothing more. Then he wrote them on two stone tablets and gave them to me.

When you heard the voice out of the darkness, while the mountain was ablaze with fire, all the leaders of your tribes and your elders came to me. And you said, "The LORD our God has shown us his glory and his majesty, and we have heard his voice from the fire. Today we have seen that a person can live even if God speaks with them. But now, why should we die? This great fire will consume us, and we will die if we hear the voice of the LORD our God any longer. For what mortal has ever heard the voice of the living God speaking out of fire, as we have, and survived? Go near and listen to all that the LORD our God says. Then tell us whatever the LORD our God tells you. We will listen and obey."

In this text, *the people of Israel specifically rule out the option that individuals could have their own sessions with God that they could then compare with that of Moses.* This alternative is considered and emphatically ruled out with the explanation that the Hebrew people had indeed heard the voice of God from the mountain and were afraid that hearing God in this way would result in their deaths. They explicitly made a deal with Moses, saying that God had continued to speak to him and he did not die, so they (the Hebrew people) would rely upon Moses alone hearing the direct self-revelation from God, and they would listen to it (read it) and obey.

A central question comes to mind: Why would the Hebrew people react this way?

I have an opinion about this. The Hebrew children had been immersed in Egyptian culture for several generations. In that culture, the pharaoh was considered God upon the earth, perfectly qualified to speak and act as God. The words and actions of the pharaoh were considered to be the literal words and actions dictated by God.

Under this cultural understanding, it was very important to keep the tradition that the pharaoh and God were indistinguishable. Why was this so important? Because the pharaoh rules as the God-king. Who needs soldiers to enforce the pharaoh's will when he is the living God?

It is reasonable to expect that this principle—the pharaoh is the living God—was so important for the governing of Egypt that any infraction was punishable by death. In other words, to attempt to interpret God's nature and will as revealed through individual, personal experience was heretical if it disagreed with the current understanding and was likely to result in death as punishment.

The text of Deuteronomy attests that the Hebrew children had just experienced this principle in action, regarding God speaking to them individually. According to their Egyptian cultural heritage, hearing the word of God in a personal way would result in death.

The text conveys that they witnessed Moses hear the literal word of God and not die. This had previously happened as Moses directly challenged the pharaoh, in his court, "Let my people go." This is the will of God. The pharaoh, of course, had a different understanding and told Moses to not show his face to him (the pharaoh) again or he would surely die.

This was the understanding the Hebrew children had of Moses. He had defied and contradicted the God-king with his own individual interpretation of divine self-revelation and lived to tell about it.

According to the Deuteronomy text, the Hebrew children had seen this as a personal message from God to Moses and considered it a sign of personal favor. They could depend on Moses to directly deal with both the pharaoh and the living God of Mount Sinai. This understanding was directly contrary to what they expected. God had shown Moses to be a reliable mediator of his will. In their Egyptian cultural perspective, they would not do the same; they would die. Thus, they made a deal with Moses: write down whatever God tells you, pass it on to us, and we will obey.

This was the bedrock upon which Judaism was founded. The texts of the Torah were considered without flaw. Potential errors of transcription were managed by having a corps of scribes specifically charged with keeping the texts uncorrupted, and the meaning of the texts was properly interpreted by learned rabbis. In this way, the people could obey the laws given, and life would be good.

There is another assumption: the preferred language God uses to speak to people is Hebrew. Thus, only Hebrew speakers (Jewish people) understand the fullness of God's self-revelation. The understanding about God gained by means of any other language is inferior.

Let me address the issue of literality first.

In my studies, it was explained to me that the story of Sodom and Gomorrah in Genesis 19:1-24 gives the basis for the Orthodox Jewish opinion that homosexuality is offensive to God and that the penalty for such behavior is death.

In that story, Lot, an inhabitant of Sodom, takes in some strangers. He is then faced with a mob that demands he surrender his guests to them. The common interpretation of these words is that the mob wants to homosexually rape the visitors. Instead, Lot pacifies the mob by offering them his daughters. Later, he and his family leave Sodom as God destroys the city in retaliation for its wickedness. This is based on the Masoretic text of the Torah, from Babylon.

I know pious Jewish people to be compassionate and loving. I asked how this laudable reputation could stand in the face of such a judgment. I was given no explanation except "This is what the Torah says, and the Torah is without blemish." Incidentally, it seemed that this was a very painful subject for the rabbi to whom I addressed the question. I considered him a man of deep spirituality and compassion.

There is an alternate explanation. The noted texts come from the Jewish religious tradition of Babylon—the people who went there in exile after the defeat of Israel by King Nebuchadnezzar. These texts are called the Masoretic texts and are considered the definitive version of the Hebrew scriptures.

I went to seminary and read different copies of the Torah and commentary, produced from outside this Babylonian Jewish community. Very ancient forms exist. One was the Samaritan Torah, which is regarded as heretical by Orthodox Jews. It was the version of the sacred texts held by the Samaritans, the Hebrew-speaking people of northern Israel who were not dispersed by the exile.

The second source I read was pieces of a Palestinian Torah and interpretation from the Dead Sea scrolls. These were texts outside of the exile experience. In this Palestinian cultural context, the noted story has God punishing the inhabitants of Sodom for not showing hospitality to the stranger. In that tradition, the mob was incensed by the fact that Lot had given strangers food and shelter.

From this background, the opinion can be rendered that interpretation of the Masoretic text had become culturally corrupted by the morals of the Babylonian Jewish community, similar to how the previous Egyptian cultural context had led the Hebrew people to a certain principle of divine authority based on the single direct revelation of God to Moses, who dictated the details of that revelation to be written down in Hebrew.

If true, this corruption does harm in two ways. First, it brings condemnation down on an entire category of people—homosexuals. Second, the Palestinian meaning is missed—the importance of hospitality to strangers. That Palestinian meaning has a very important message for people in our current day who would deny refugees relief from their perils.

These things are not some recent vain invention of my imagination. Other Hebrew and Christian scriptures back up my opinion on this subject, such as the story of the tower of Babel (Genesis 11:1-9) as well as Acts 2:8, which talks about God communicating to diverse sets of people, each in their own language. Nobody owns the right to speak for God because of their ethnicity.

Even so, the presumption that someone living in an entirely different culture many centuries later can say, "This is what the writer really meant," is madness. Whose alternate meaning shall we accept? On what basis? It's just another form of cultural contamination.

I acknowledge that there is the danger of chaos if free-form correction of sacred texts is allowed. The antidote is reasoned, respectful debate based on personal experience together with prayer to God for inspiration and guidance.

There is a modern-day error that says we are to decouple religion from our national life. This is wrong! We are to decouple partisan religion (spirituality) from corrupting our lives. What I've written about is a human treasure, although I have experienced much (but not all) of it through a Christian cultural perspective.

The use of personal experience to confirm the truth of what is written is a good antidote to continued cultural contamination of the truth affirmed by human experience.

We do it the way our forbears did, through prayer, inspiration, discernment, and reasoned debate.

As an important aside, this is a modern-day political problem also. The United States has a sacred text (the Constitution) that was written long ago. That document does not directly address many things that have happened in the centuries since it was written.

One clear example of this is the authority of the US president to take the country to war without the constitutional authority of the people voting to do so through their elected representatives in Congress. The text has been reinterpreted in light of the post-World War II threat of nuclear attack, which did not allow the luxury of gathering Congress before reacting. There wasn't time.

Instead of revising the Constitution with an amendment after careful debate, we work around the problem, with each presidential administration making its own interpretation to suit its fancy based on the issue of raw political power instead of reasoned, logical debate based on shared experience. Acting in this way often has severe unintended consequences that show up in the future.

What's the solution? There's one to both types of problems: put God into the equation.

The founding fathers of our country were people of faith. They knew how to pray and directly solicited the aid of God in their deliberations. I know this from more than history books (which are vulnerable to politically corrupt individuals spinning the truth for latter-day personal advantage). Why do I say this? I am a direct relative (on my father's side) of many of those people—a colonial governor, the first president of the Continental Congress, and four subsequent US presidents. I know the family stories, and I have read their writings.

The answer to both problems is to put God into the equation. Counter the threat of unintended consequences by prayerful deliberation that builds upon prior logical experience-based discussion but that makes specific provision for divine inspiration.

Do this nationally as well as personally using the process Jesus teaches us in scripture.

Chapter Three

KENOSIS—WHAT IS IT AND WHY IS IT IMPORTANT TO US?

Kenosis is a Greek word. In a broad sense, it means "to be emptied." It has an important place in Orthodox Christian theology, in the area of Christology—the theology of who Christ is, his work, and the meaning of his life.

Put simply, it refers to the idea that God "emptied himself" and encountered people as a living, breathing human being like us with his incarnation as Jesus.

Why is this important?

As discussed in the introduction to this book, we humans are limited in our capabilities, and those capabilities are not equal to the task of carrying out our good intentions. Sometimes (most times?) we are not strong enough, wise enough, or caring enough to be more precise.

We feel guilty and often look to shift the blame for the bad results to others when things turn out badly.

Let me repeat a critical paragraph from the introduction, because it is key to understanding this chapter: We are angry with God for making us the imperfect creatures that we are. God has given us guidance in the form of religious teachings on how to speak and act to avoid contributing to those disasters, but our humanity limits us in putting that guidance into effect. The anger focuses on a critical question: Why create us as flawed creatures and tell us how to live, knowing that we are not capable of carrying out that guidance?

Why is living by the God-given religious texts not enough?

The incarnation of Jesus and the concept of kenosis helps put this into perspective. Why did we need Jesus? A credible answer is to help us deal with the anger and resentment toward God that I just mentioned.

The idea is that God emptied himself in the form of Jesus. He did it so that we could learn by example how a human with limited capabilities can ask, receive, and carry out God's guidance and grace on how to speak and act to make this world a better place. This doesn't work if Jesus is "superior" to us. Jesus has to be a real, hungry, thirsty, tired, horny, cranky human being, not some remote, nonhuman fantasy.

Let me give you a practical example to bring the point home. During the 1960s, at the height of the civil rights movement, there were many zealous activists from Northern states who drove down to places like Mississippi and Alabama to protest racial discrimination. They confronted the local authorities about their unjust laws and practices.

There was a backlash to all this. The backlash came in the form of violence and recrimination by certain white factions toward the black citizens of those locales.

In turn, experiencing those difficulties created a sense of resentment among those black people. They had to bear the backlash while the activists could return to the North to their safe houses and societies, where they bore no adverse consequences for the movements they had helped instigate.

Simply put, they had no kenosis! Their actions instigated strife that others then had to deal with. The agitators did not have to bear the consequences of their actions. Others bore the consequences for them.

It would have been more appropriate, and more fitting, if all those Northern agitators had stayed around and borne the consequences. Then there would have been less resentment from local blacks. That, of course, was difficult or impossible. Some brave souls stuck around and bore the brutal, sometimes fatal, consequences along with their brothers and sisters. The experience of this adversity was often different depending on a person's skin color. For some whites, their "whiteness" still gave them some measure of protection that their black colleagues did not enjoy. This is one aspect of what is called "white privilege."

Instead, what the movement needed were local black leaders. They needed a black "Jesus," not a white one.

Someone who lived that calling was Dr. Martin Luther King Jr. As a black minister, he exemplified the teachings of God through his words and actions, and he paid the martyr's price for doing so—the same price his blessed Lord Jesus paid. He was the modern-day manifestation of a black Jesus. He took the teachings and example of Jesus and applied them in his life, but Jesus showed him the way.

This is what we have to do to resolve the problem of evil and injustice in our society. We must put our good intentions to work so that, together with God, we can and will build his kingdom on this earth. We can copy Jesus and learn from his teachings and example. We can learn how to do what he did—discern the will of our heavenly Father in our particular lives and use prayer to ask for and use the grace God provides in response to our prayer request so that we can carry out His will for us and through us.

Exactly how we do that will be addressed later in this book, but this is what we are called to do, to continue and complete the work that Jesus started more than two thousand years ago. Understand, however, that pleading the limitations of our humanity to avoid the burden of living the life won't work. God, by his act of kenosis in the incarnation of Jesus, showed us what a normal human being could do when he or she depends upon God for guidance and grace to carry through the work to its perfection. No excuses! As Jesus puts it in the Sermon on the Mount, as quoted in the Gospel of Matthew, "Be ye perfect as your Father in Heaven is perfect" (Matthew 5:48).

In this context, Jesus is talking about love for one another in the sense of God's love for all his children. Jesus is urging people to become, by their loving, like their Father in heaven. In other words, become complete and finished in your love, not restricted or partial. And that most certainly does not imply that we are capable of being flawless or sinless.

In the full context of Jesus's life and work, we are taught to become the perfected, completed person that God intends each of us to be. Thus, we need to learn to walk with God and look to him for the guidance and grace we need. We need to be good in our thoughts, words, and deeds rather than flawed and therefore erroneous because of our individual human inadequacies.

Thus, learning to walk with the Lord is to team with him. We are an action element that puts God's inspiration and strength into play to achieve his good will on this earth. We, who are visible, therefore manifest the character of our Father in heaven, who is invisible. We are loving children of a loving Father. The apple doesn't fall far from the tree, as the saying goes.

Each year, on his special holiday, I often think of Brother Martin Luther King Jr. as one of God's perfected. His goal wasn't tolerance but reconciliation, loving our Lord Jesus and loving one another as our heavenly Father loves each of us.

I close this chapter with one of the few examples of the Aramaic language, the language of Jesus, in our Bible: "If there is anyone who does not love the Lord, such a one is living under a curse. Maranatha [Come Lord]" (1 Corinthians 16:22)! Heal your children of this curse of incomplete, unfinished love.

Chapter Four

THE BENEFITS
OF THE WALK

Discussions in previous chapters centered on this question: What is righteousness? Simply put, it is walking the right path for each of us, being ruled by God. This chapter focuses on a key issue: Why is it important to live righteously?

First, let's address the matter of "partial" righteousness. Suppose I'm not on the right path all the time. What happens to the benefits? Do I get none of the benefits without perfection, some of them, or all of them in a partial sense, proportional to the degree to which I'm on the right path? Before I address these questions, let me tell you about the benefits.

First of all, there is joy. This is a pleasant "feeling" that is built into us as we strive to walk with the Lord. This is a partial benefit because it is a "homing beacon" sort of thing. Its purpose is to tell you that at the moment you are feeling the joy, you are on the path of righteousness. Conversely, if you are not feeling the joy, you are "off the beam," so to speak. Joy is the central feeling that we must use to walk the walk. Without such a "sensor," we could never gain the ability to walk with God.

Jesus talks about this when he says, "The Father and I are one" (John 1:27-30). He is talking about demonstrating how he is in a continuous state of alignment with God and that this is also available to us as we grow in our ability to recognize and follow God's guidance.

Actually, righteousness is the diametric opposite of sin. The canonical definition of sin is to not be right with God. Indeed, the Greek word in the Gospels for sin is *hamartia*. This was originally an archery term that meant "to miss the mark." It was adopted in the church because it so clearly illustrates the nature of sin—not being one with God, not being righteous. It didn't matter how far you were off the mark (the bull's-eye). Only hitting the bull's-eye counted.

We feel joy when we love and are loved. This tells us something about the prime benefit of walking with God. Being righteous, in this way, is the central purpose in life for human beings. As I will explain more in later chapters, we are fully grown in our ability to love when we are able to love as God does. This is a direct command from Jesus to each one of us: "Be ye perfect, as your father in heaven is perfect." (Matthew 5:48). The Greek gospel word *(teleioi)* usually translated as "perfect" more accurately means "finished, completed."

By this reasoning, if we have attained righteousness (but not sinlessness), we should be in a continual state of joy. Make no mistake; Jesus is telling us that, unlike sinlessness, becoming loving like God is attainable by each one of us.

What about sin? Being righteous means being freed from the burden of sin. When we walk with God and are one with God, we are righteous. God supplies each of us 24-7, 365 with the guidance and grace to not hurt others unintentionally, because of our built-in human limitations. This is the "evil" we specifically pray to be delivered from in the Lord's Prayer.

Otherwise, when we are in a state of sin, we are incredibly burdened by the responsibility to not hurt others unintentionally while knowing from our limited nature that we cannot avoid doing so without God's help.

This is the second major benefit of walking the walk: peace, relief from our burdens of guilt. The capacity for feeling unease due to imperfection is also built into us as another indicator that will lead us to seek the divine path, flee from the pain of imperfection and the anxiety, and seek the pleasure of joy. The Bible phrase that applies is, "Come unto me, all ye that travail and are heavy burdened, and I will give you rest" (Matthew 1:28-29). Incidentally, this is why twelve-step programs to recover from addiction emphasize the need for belief in a greater power if such programs are to work.

A major reason for addictions to alcohol or drugs is that they manipulate the chemistry of the body to ease the pangs of imperfection I am talking about.

More traditionally, we can summarize the benefits of walking with the Lord as the "fruits of the Spirit" (Galatians 5:22-23). They are love, joy, peace, forbearance, kindness, goodness, faithfulness, gentleness, and self-control.

Chapter Five

WALKING IN LOVE: THE PROCESS

Previous chapters have developed the assertion that Jesus brought a new perspective to religion. This new perspective is that individual human beings are capable of direct contact and inspiration from God on a constant basis. This capability can be acquired by good intention and development, and the fruits that result are a joyful, fulfilled life. Let us now focus on the process by which we are to reach the goal of righteousness.

WALKING THE WALK

To walk such a walk requires that each individual think and act within the context of a certain set of beliefs. Those four core beliefs are as follows:

1. God is good - loving and gracious who wants only the best for us.

2. God communicates with us through his presence within us and around us.

3. Love is our primary calling as human beings—love of God, our neighbors, and ourselves.

4. We should always choose life over death, living fully with as much joy as possible, whatever the circumstance.

These are presented as a summary figure - Figure 11, Walking in Love - The Building-Block Beliefs that Enable It:

Ultimately, we must be convinced these beliefs are true by our own personal experience. The belief must be true, not feigned, or the process will not work and a "process of pretense" might actually harm us.

---

[1]   I am indebted to John Roberto for this succinct way of presenting these principles in his publication, Living Well—Christian Practices for Everyday Life (Lifelong Faith Associates, 2009).

Sometimes people are given a big gift, often called the "beatific vision" or "an encounter with the risen Lord." This is a direct encounter with the "energies" of God. Such an experience often comes during a life crisis where there is a real life-or-death choice, and the person heroically chooses life. This simple choice triggers the encounter with God that confirms belief number four and provides all the rest of the belief elements noted above.

Saint Paul had such an experience, as did acknowledged saints of the church and many others we never hear about.

Figure 1: Walking in Love- The Building Block Beliefs That Enable It

1. God Is Good ~ loving and gracious who wants only the best for us.

2. God Communicates with Us - through His presence within us and around us.

3. Love Is Our Primary Calling as Human Beings - love of God, our neighbor and ourselves.

4. Choose Life Over Death - live fully, with as much joy as possible, whatever the circumstance.

ULTIMATELY, WE MUST BE CONVINCED THESE ARE TRUE BY OUR OWN PERSONAL EXPERIENCE

When such an epiphany happens, many people who are conventional Christians don't talk about it. They fear this is some kind of heresy, but it is not. It is at the center of the Christian faith. In such a direct divine encounter, all four elements of the belief system necessary to walk with the Lord are provided in one fell swoop. The experience immediately equips such a person for this walk for the rest of his or her life. It also leaves a mark. People who encounter the person sense a charisma they can't explain.

Note, however, that such an experience is not the focus of what I'm writing about or promising. Why do some people have such an immediate experience and others do not? Who knows? Maybe they're proving by witness that such a capability exists. For the rest, the necessary belief structure needs to be developed in a more conventional way. Explaining that process is the subject of the rest of this chapter and the next two chapters that follow.

BUILDING TRUST IN THE GOODNESS OF GOD

To learn to walk the walk, you need to gain experience. It is this experience that will convince you, over time, of the truth of beliefs one through three. Belief number four is the first and critical one. Death is the certain end to all uncertain future possibilities. You need to achieve belief number four through discipline. Always choose life over death. This is not just physical life and death but also spiritual life and death in the here and now. Jesus sums it up: "I come that they may have life, and have it more abundantly" (John 10:10). One of the interpretations in the original Greek text uses "going beyond all expectations" as the precursor phrase often translated into English as "abundantly."

So how do we gain the experience? A piece of good news is that it doesn't have to be just your own experience. You can benefit from the experiences of others, so you don't have to go through everything from scratch.

As you progress, you will be challenged constantly by your own ego, the part of you that wants to control what you do so that you think your way through life, so to speak. This is spiritually deadly. Such an approach guarantees a failed life. Your ego opposes you through fear and anxiety.

You need to get past this. Jesus says, "Be not anxious. Can any of you extend the span of your life by one hour by being anxious? (Matthew 6:25-27)"

Regarding fear, you soon learn that all or most of your conscious fears are illusions. When confronted, they vanish. There are things you should fear, but the ones that are surprises are the ones that get you.

How can a person deal with fear and anxiety? Think about something you would like to do but are fearful or anxious about trying. Instead of running away or pretending the fear doesn't exist, ask yourself, "What is the worst that might happen if I turn and face my fear?" If you can afford the worst happening, do it. Take a bite of life. Take a controlled risk. See what happens. It doesn't have to be a big bite; just a nibble will do.

If it turns out well, take another bite. If it doesn't, don't give up. Learn from the pluses and minuses at your own pace. You've got a whole lifetime to work this out.

COMMUNICATING WITH GOD

As you walk this walk of gaining experience, ask God to help. He will give you the wisdom and strength you need to succeed.

Don't worry if the things you ask for seem trivial. This is a learning exercise. As you ask God for things, you are guaranteed that God will give them to you as long as they are not harmful to you or others. This builds confidence. You learn that God gives you what you ask for, albeit at his own time and in his own way.

Also, don't worry if you misunderstand what God is communicating. God will persist until you understand the message correctly.

This point is made clear in a famous story about Saint Francis of Assisi. Francis was from a well-off Italian family and had been a soldier. He turned from that profession when he received God's communication to him: "Francis, build my church." Francis then gathered some of his friends from the neighborhood and worked on rebuilding an old church that had gone into ruin, stone by stone.

When Francis was at prayer, God kept repeating the same communication: "Build my church." At some point, Francis became exasperated and complained to God, "God, why do you keep saying that when we're doing everything we can to follow your wishes?"

Finally, in his exasperation, Francis got it. God wanted him to build his church as a movement, not rebuild a physical church.

This is the fear of the convinced, then. We fear, like Francis, that we are misunderstanding the guidance God has sent in answer to our prayers.

Note, however, that God clarifies the communication by persistence.

Also, God answering your prayers in his own time and in his own way is important. You will find that God has a wicked sense of humor.

I'll illustrate with a fanciful but symbolically illustrative story. Once upon a time, a poor scavenger was walking along the beach of one of the islands of the Caribbean. A luxury resort was on the ridge above the beach. Beautiful people were eating beautiful food, drinking beautiful beverages, listening to beautiful music, and having a beautiful time. The scavenger thought, *I could be up there and be one of them if only I had money.*

Shortly after having that thought, he noticed a bottle washed up in the sand. He went over to it and rubbed the sand away so he could read the label. All of a sudden, a genie popped out and said, "Boy, am I happy to get out of that little bottle. An evil wizard put me in it. As a reward, I'll grant you three wishes."

Quickly, the scavenger said, "I'd like a thousand bucks." Instantly, a thousand male deer appeared on the beach. The scavenger complained to the genie, "That's not what I wanted. I wanted money."

The genie replied, "You got what you said you wanted. You have to be a little more careful of what you wish for."

God has done the equivalent to me quite often. I don't get angry. It just makes God more real to me and helps me love him for his cornball humor.

All progress in this kind of spiritual work depends on the belief (supported by experience) that God communicates with us. It does take a bit of training to learn to recognize the Master's voice. John's Gospel talks about this: "My sheep know my voice. I call them and they follow me" (John 10:5).

I have no experience of this in a literal sense and once tended to pooh-pooh such a communication process, but my opinion changed a few years ago when I met a retired

Methodist minister who said God spoke to him in words when he was ten years old and told him he wanted him to become a pastor. This particular person had a celebrated career over the span of many years in rural eastern Maryland. The wonderful lifelong career attests to the validity of his testimony. That experience now makes me even more cautious about making dogmatic statements about how God communicates.

Even so, the more typical communication I'm familiar with is unspoken. For example, if you experience an entire string of seemingly unrelated, unlikely coincidences, it is usually an indication that God is speaking to you (in a symbolic sense) through those events. Also, you get used to sensing something in your gut that tips you off. However the communication happens, a person must believe such communication is possible in order to walk with the Lord in the biblical sense. You pray to God, and God answers your prayer. Skill in listening to God comes with experience.

A common starting point in establishing one's ability to "hear" God is through dreams. I was once trained as a Jungian therapist (a disciple of the Swiss psychiatrist Carl Jung). In that training, we were taught to explore our ability to receive communications from our interior channel by paying careful attention to our dreams. It was fascinating.

If you were struggling with some problem or situation, you thought about it as you were falling asleep. You put a notepad by the side of your bed so that when you awoke, you could immediately record your dreams before you forgot them. This simple act of taking the dream channel seriously kicked off a new learning path for me.

I'll give you a true example, including the ubiquitous cornball humor of God to which I previously referred.

I was struggling to understand how I was going to get through a particular life challenge. I then got this high-fidelity, stereo-sound, living-color dream. For me, such aspects present in a dream are an immediate tip-off that the dream is important.

I was aboard a navy aircraft carrier that was steaming, unruffled, through a raging storm toward port. The details of the dream were strange. Everywhere I looked, a relative was popping out of a hatch or through a door. I sort of understood that, somehow, this ship was going to carry me safely through my troubles, which were signified by the storm. The problem was I didn't know what the dream meant.

I remained puzzled for weeks until I was having lunch with a friend and describing the dream to her. Frustrated, I said, "I don't understand what kind of ship this is that's going to save me."

In a flash, the answer popped into my head. This was a "relationship." It was my close relationship with the US Navy that was going to bail me out.

THE RESULT OF THIS "TESTING" EXPERIENCE

There's another thing that happens in this process of asking and receiving, questioning and learning. After God gave me what I asked for, I would realize that it wasn't what I really needed. After many years of this, I got the point. God always gives me what I ask for, as long as it's not going to be bad for me or others. Over the years, this has built up my confidence in belief number one: God is good. It also teaches me that I don't know what's good for me, but God does. Except for occasional lapses, I stopped asking for specific things.

Instead, I now say, "I trust you to give me what I really need: my daily bread."

What might that daily bread be? It's belief number three. God had been silently, secretly growing me to be more and more loving. The more joy I got out of life, the more I loosened up and the more loving I became.

THE RESULTS OF THE PROCESS

The process I've described was not only about building confidence in the goodness of the Lord. In parallel, God was working away within me to give me "the Pearl of Great Price," to transform me into the loving creature he intended me to be.

It is the opposite of being perfect in an egotistical, self-centered way. It doesn't mean I am without flaws or sin. It is precisely because of those limitations that I trust God to guide me and give me the grace to carry out that guidance. I work as a member of his team (whenever he calls me to participate). This is the way all humans are designed to work in this world he created, and sustains by his nonvisible presence. It is a continuing work.

The other result is more permanent, a way of being. God taught me the primacy of love as his calling to all of us and that we are each able to become perfected (completed) in this calling. That is the subject of the next chapter.

Chapter Six

THE PRIMACY OF LOVE IN HUMAN LIFE

Preceding chapters have developed the theme that Jesus brought humanity a new revelation regarding the nature of God and how humans are to relate to him to their great benefit. It did not negate previous revelations but extended and deepened them.

The new dimension that was added was the necessity for humans to become perfected in order to achieve their potential in life. This new dimension is called walking with the Lord.

Why is this so?

First refer to the unique role Jesus was to play in our world. We've already talked about how Jesus shows, by his life and work, how we ordinary humans can walk with the Lord. Such teachings enable us to carry out certain features and functions of our design as human beings. Such a walk is necessary because we are not intended to successfully make our way through life by living as independent, limited, creatures. This doesn't mean we are bad by nature. It only says we are designed to work and live connected to a greater power that provides us the wisdom and power we otherwise lack.

There is another design function of human beings that is not limited: the ability to love. Jesus, in the Sermon on the Mount, commands us to "Be ye perfect as your Father in heaven is perfect" (Matthew 5:48). In the context of the text before and after this quoted verse, Jesus is talking about the love of God for his creation. Jesus then sets us a new goal for life, to become perfect. The Greek word for "perfect" in the original gospel manuscripts (teleioi) is better translated as "finished" or "completed" rather than the implication of being Godlike, except in one way, by our love.

Why is this different from our flaws and imperfections, our so- called human failings? It is because we are also given a capability to grow in our love. This is effected by the experience of feeling joy more and more as we grow in our ability to conform ourselves, more and more, to God's good will for us.

Why is this so? When we love, we experience joy as a consequence. Another human being who is the object of our love also experiences joy at the same time. That person senses that he or she is loved and is designed to respond in two ways. The first way is to feel joy at being loved. The second way is to respond to the feeling of being loved by loving back. This provides an additional sense of joy.

This functionality is built into us from our conception. The only "fall" (in the Augustinian view of human inclination towards sinfulness) lies in somehow forgetting that we had that capability or in losing it. Otherwise, humans are designed to function as agents as well as recipients of love. We see this in small children and babies.

Why do I say this?

I love babies. I always have, and I get worse with age. When I see a baby in the grocery store or at the mall, I have a compulsion to go talk to him or her. I speak to the baby in baby talk and say how beautiful he or she is and talk to specific points of the baby's beauty, such as his or her hair, eyes, and so on. The baby responds with a smile or a giggle or does a happy kick. In short, the baby feels the love and returns it.

I do this because it feels good to love. A baby returns love in kind because it also feels good to do so. In other words, love is designed into us at the level of instinct. The good feeling we experience when we love or are loved has a name. Joy! We are built so that we get a reward—the feeling of joy—whenever we love. This reward keeps us doing the desired behavior. Loving is somehow important in how we and the world are designed. We are supposed to love. Why?

We are designed to love because love has a positive role to play in the way the world operates. Love has a redeeming and therapeutic benefit to the world. Without love, there is unredeemed and unhealed hurt.

This doesn't just happen with humans. We also see it in other creatures, such as dogs. Puppies respond to being loved just like babies do, but unlike babies, dogs never seem to lose their capability to love. Let me illustrate this with a personal story.

I'm a dog person. I especially love puppies. With puppies, I talk to them, tickle their bellies, scratch them behind the ears, and generally show them love. Just like babies, they immediately respond by loving me back. They lick my face, which is how doggies show love.

When my boys were growing up, we had a succession of doggies —two Saint Bernards and then a Welsh Corgi. We picked up the Corgi from the breeder in 1976—the bicentennial year of the Republic. In honor of that occasion, the breeder had given each puppy the name of a Revolutionary War character—Molly Pitcher, Light Horse Harry, Patrick Henry, and so on. We immediately chose Patrick Henry to take home.

Like all puppies, when you first separate them from their moms and brothers and sisters, they are sad and weep. They miss the love. Patrick was no exception. He cried all evening. I didn't go to bed that night but instead sat up all night in the recliner with Patrick on my shoulder so he could feel the warmth of my body and the beat of my heart. After several hours, he stopped crying, and we both fell asleep. I awoke hours later with Patrick licking my face. He was okay! My love for him had taught him that he was now in a human family who loved him. He responded with love to a new life with his new human family. It's the doggie way!

Think of this. In the world as God designed it, he provided for cross-species love, and in some ways, doggie love is superior to human love. Humans have a nasty habit of sometimes betraying or abandoning those whom they love. Doggies never do this. They are steadfast to the end.

Now let me illustrate how humans sometimes seem to lose the capacity to love that they once had or the concept of which they are (at least) confused by.

The confusion factor seems to be especially prevalent in our culture with many guys. Some guys hate the word *love*! To those guys, it seems to signal some sort of entrapment. Let me give you an example with a true story.

A few years ago, I was in a relationship with a really nice guy. We were very compatible. Two things about him were especially endearing. First, he was so gentle. Whenever he spoke or acted toward another person, he did so with an acute gentleness—a consideration that takes into account how the other person might respond.

He also had a loving heart that shined forth in all his thoughts and deeds. To me, he was a real prince of a guy. How could a person not love him?

One day, we were sitting around and, on impulse, I said, "Joe [not his real name; I don't want to embarrass him], I love you, babe!"

He replied, "Don't say that!"

I said, "You mean the L-word? Love, love, love, love, love!"

He replied, "Stop saying that. I don't like that word!"

I then said, "I guess this means you don't love me!"

He said, "I didn't say that! I like you. Actually, I really, really, really like you an awful, awful, awful lot!"

"So you like me a really, really, really, awful, awful, awful lot, but you don't love me? That must be why you call me once or twice a day to talk. You like me a really, really, really, awful, awful, awful lot, but you don't love me."

He said, "That's right! You got it right."

Of course he loved me. He was just confused about what words to use to describe his behavior or was fearful that admitting his love might lock him into some sort of undesired obligation.

A couple of days later, during one of our telephone calls, he said, "You know that discussion we were having the other day? I thought about what you said, and I want you to know I love you, baby!"

I replied, "I know you do, but thanks for saying so."

You see, the loss or confusion is not irretrievable. All we need to do is remember to focus on our feelings and chase the rush of feeling joyful. We need to practice this until we are able to love all human beings the same way God does, without distinction. If and when we get to that point, we are perfected in the gospel sense.

Jesus speaks of this in the Gospel of Matthew. He uses the discussion to emphasize this commonality between humans and God with regard to love. He uses an analogy between the behavior of a loving parent toward a child and the love of God. "Which of you, if your child asks for a loaf of bread, would give that child a stone? Which of you, if your child asked for a piece of fish, would give them a serpent? If you, then, being a doer of evil, know how to give good gifts to your children, how much more will your Father in heaven give good gifts to those who ask him" (Matthew 2:9-11)?

These stories are important because people can see and feel the love of another human being or a puppy, but sometimes they cannot sense the direct love of God very well. Scripture tells us that God is love. When we humans advertise ourselves as the children of an invisible God, our loving behavior teaches others that when we love, we are simply reflecting the love of the heavenly Father who made us. Simply put, our loving behavior is a critical part of God's self-revelation to humanity as to who he is.

Let me now tell you a true Christmas story that bears upon the issue of love and its power to bring peace.

A few years ago, I flew east to spend Christmas with my sons. The plane tickets during the holidays were so expensive that I had to fly the red-eye from Los Angeles to Baltimore on Christmas morning to be able to afford the trip. It was about 5:00 a.m. I picked up my bag and waited to give my youngest son the chance to sleep a little longer before he came and picked me up at the airport.

I was waiting alongside a Pakistani family—a young father and mother, her mother, and their two children, one very small and the other about three years old. I was sitting beside the grandmother, who spoke no English. I speak none of the languages of Pakistan, but I talked to her anyway about her beautiful grandchildren and her lovely daughter. She understood perfectly and talked back to me about her love for them and about how proud she was of them.

To pass the time, as I am often inclined to do when I see a beautiful child, I caught the baby's attention and started playing peekaboo with her. She got into it with me immediately and giggled and wiggled as I told her how beautiful she was.

After a while, I thought I should give her older sister some attention, so I tried to engage her, but whenever I looked at her, she hid herself from my view. She was wary of this strange lady.

I then struck up a conversation with her mother, who spoke English quite well. I commiserated with her about the burden she was bearing for the family on such a long trip, while her husband had gone off desperately seeking some transportation for the family from the airport. She acknowledged that the trip had been a challenge for her.

It seemed clear to me that they were not very familiar with the United States and its customs, so they had not anticipated what early Christmas morning was like and how hard it would be to find transportation.

After seeing all of this, the older child changed her attitude. She now figured that the strange lady was not so strange after all, so she came to me carrying her stuffed parrot of many colors and started telling me about herself and her parrot.

After a while, the husband finally came back, having successfully found some transportation.

As they departed, I gave the mom and her mother each a big hug, and the three-year-old also came up to get her hug. I said, "Good luck!" and waved goodbye.

What a beautiful gift God gave me on that Christmas morning—an opportunity to use my love to ease their fears of being strangers in a strange land. This spontaneous happening totally changed the situation. They now knew that at least one of the people in this country was just like them, a person who gave love and warmly accepted their love in return. Thus, there must be more like me. Maybe this was not such a strange land after all. This brought them peace at a difficult time.

What power this love thing has!

When we imitate the loving behavior of our heavenly Father, we are following in the footsteps of Jesus, who demonstrated the magnificent enormity of his love for us by dying on the cross so that we might live. This is the second critical aspect of why we needed Jesus to come into the world, to demonstrate how ordinary human beings can act lovingly like their Father in heaven.

This is the argument that convinces us that love is our primary calling. We are built to love God and one another because we are given the gift, at conception, of being able to feel joy. Then life experience chasing that feeling grows us in our ability to love until each one of us becomes perfected in the gospel sense.

Human love and divine love are just two sides of the same coin. It doesn't come in flavors. I think this is what Jesus (the example of the perfected person) is saying in John 10:30: "The Father and I are one."

Let me close this chapter with another story from an earlier phase of my life that shows how God grows us in our capacity to love.

It was the early 1990s, the end of the Cold War. I was living in Los Angeles at the time and was a program manager in the company called TRW. I was growing weary of doing defense work without an imminent Soviet threat to motivate me.

I prayed to God for guidance as to what I should do. Then someone told me about a local hospital that had an excellent program of training and using hospice care volunteers. They asked if I had ever considered doing such a thing. No, I said, but I immediately got in touch with the hospital. Maybe I could do a pious act and learn from the experience.

The training was excellent. They then put us to work as caring companions for patients who were approaching death. Our job was to visit the people, get to know them, listen to them, and generally be there for them so they didn't feel so totally alone and abandoned. Many of them had been abandoned by their families or had no surviving family or friends to visit them.

Even under the best of circumstances, what was happening to these patients was cruel (not because of what the facility could do but because of what it could not do). Here were human beings, many of whom had lost their sense of dignity and humanity. When they looked at themselves in a mirror, they often did not recognize themselves because of the ravages of disease and the aging process. They were connected to tubes and wires and often were incontinent or just generally smelled bad.

I understood my job. I was to be there for them to ease their feelings of helplessness and abandonment and try to help them get back some part of their humanity and self-respect. Otherwise, I had no therapeutic function. That was up to God. My greatest qualification for doing this, besides having had the training, was that I was notably not squeamish about the unpleasant physical side of humanity. Babies, old people—it's all the same.

Then something wonderful happened. As I got to know the person, something welled up from deep within me. I was amazed to discover I had this previously unnoticed capacity to love in an incredibly powerful way. This was totally unexpected but tremendously fulfilling and joyful. Can you understand how thrilling it is to discover something like that abides inside us, just waiting to be awakened by the touch of the Lord under the right circumstances?

I could see the real person through all the outer barriers. I could hold their hands and give them the touch of another human being that humans are so often hungry for. I could even bend over and kiss them on their foreheads when that seemed appropriate.

My first patient began to really look forward to my visits. She sensed the love and began to return it in small ways. A smile of joy and a sparkle in her eyes were the tip-offs.

God had answered my prayer and was using the opportunity to teach me something about the capacity each of us, as human beings, has to grow in our ability to love.

So many benefits flowed from that experience. It equipped me to help my own mom when the time came to navigate through these aging challenges. It also led me to enter seminary and embark upon a new career in pastoral care ministry.

This was why I subsequently spent five years in a parish in Baltimore, Maryland, as Lay Vicar and pastoral care minister.

I tell you this story because it shows, by example, what I'm talking about when I say "walk in love." God answered my prayer for a new career focus, and in the process he gave me a quantum leap forward in unleashing my human potential to love. God was perfecting me in the terms I previously discussed.

Chapter Seven

CHOOSING LIFE OVER DEATH

The subject of this chapter is the fourth of the four essential beliefs I mentioned that are necessary for someone to live a fulfilled life, one of spiritual unity with God, the creator and sustainer of life, which, among other things, is the life force behind our very existence.

I want to expand upon the title by telling a true story from my own life experience that shows why belief number four is so important. First, though, I want to let you know what the story will tell you and what to look for.

The major theme is simple. In times of distress, there can be great temptation to end one's life. This point occurs when a person feels hopeless. You just want the misery to end. Killing yourself can most certainly achieve that goal. The problem is that by terminating your life, you will end the misery, but you will also forestall future possibilities your human limitations prevent you from foreseeing.

Those possibilities could be as simple as a medical breakthrough or a proper diagnosis and treatment in the face of uncertain health issues.

Here's the story about me to illustrate the point.

About sixteen years ago, I suffered a severe heart attack. As a result of the damage, my heart would stop beating but then eventually start back up. When it stopped, the feeling was very unpleasant. It was the dying feeling! I can't describe it to you, but I can tell you that every cell in my body seemed to recognize it. When —not if—you experience it, you will know exactly what it is.

The doctors tried everything they knew to fix the problem. First it was stents and then heart bypass surgery and then electric shock therapy, and finally they put in a pacemaker that made me dependent upon it to live. Nothing worked.

In the meantime, I was in a state of severe anxiety. I walked around never knowing when the next incident would happen. My body hated the dying feeling. It was like being waterboarded. My ego would cause me to flinch whenever it (always erroneously) anticipated an event was coming on, but it couldn't predict the event, so I walked around in a continued state of anxiety, living on tranquilizers.

The doctors told me that there was nothing else they could do for me and that I should put my affairs in order because eventually my heart would stop and not restart and that would be the end.

In my despair, I frantically searched for any possibility. One day, I found a medical paper on the internet that talked about an experimental new surgical procedure that seemed to address my problem.

I showed the paper to my Baltimore cardiologist, who was a good man. He put it before the practice of his fellow cardiologists. They concluded that, yes, it might work for me, but they could not perform the surgery. It was too risky. Too risky for them. They had never done such a procedure before and had neither the training nor the specialized tools needed to perform it. All of this was on top of the significant risk of death on the operating table that was inherent in the procedure. Well, it may have been too risky for them, but it wasn't for me. I chose the possibility of life over the certainty of death.

They contacted the author of the paper, who had developed the procedure and was then resident at the Cleveland Clinic, and shared the details of my case with him. They told me that he thought I might be a perfect candidate and had asked when I could go to Cleveland and be examined.

I was there two days later. The doctor confirmed everything and recommended immediate surgery the next morning, before my heart failed. We talked about the risk, and he told me that they had a way to handle it.

The procedure involved them repairing my heart from within by going in through incisions in both thighs with a light, a camera, a burning (ablation) tool, a snippy (cutting) tool, and a skin-resistance measurement tool to map out electrical paths.

They would use these tools to burn and snip away scar tissue and then use the other tools to map out the bad electrical paths that had developed and close them off by ablation. The risk was of killing healthy tissue or making a mistake and shutting off an essential electrical path.

That risk was managed by having me awake and lucid through the entire nine hours so that if I felt the angina (heart attack precursor feeling) coming up, I'd let them know and they would back off. Even so, the surgery was daunting— nine hours on the table, conscious but strapped down as they worked away. I tell you this so that you understand how deeply motivated I was to hold onto life. Every cell in my body was screaming, "Go for the life!" and I was listening.

It worked! A few hours after the surgery was completed, they checked me out, told me everything looked good, and sent me home the next day. Since then, I've had no more heart stoppage.

There was a price to pay, however. I was going to live but as a semi-invalid. I had lost my stamina. Even so, the government was wonderful. They wanted to have me continue my work, so they contracted with me to continue to form my teams of experts and manage them out of my home. I only needed to come in to government facilities for special reasons or for meetings, which I could manage.

I did this until about five years ago, when my California cardiologist told me the latest tests showed that my heart was now healed, aided by the drugs and proper medical treatment, and was now pumping blood totally within normal limits. I could now do anything I wanted, within my physical capabilities. I asked why I was still so weak? He said they had thought it was due to residual heart damage, but that was not true. He advised me to talk to a good endocrinologist (specialist in hormones).

I did so. The new doctor who examined me did a whole slew of blood tests and gave me a new diagnosis. I had a serious autoimmune disorder that I had probably had from well before birth. My body was at war with itself, sometimes mistaking healthy cells for alien matter and then using my immune system to attack and destroy those cells.

Over the years, it had attacked my thyroid function, gradually destroying my body's ability to convert the output of my thyroid gland (T4) into the form (T3) my body needs to use for its daily energy needs. This aspect of the disorder is called Hashimoto's disease, and I had a very severe case of it.

The doctor told me the autoimmune disorder was incurable but that the Hashimoto's disease aspect of it was certainly treatable. He gave me a little gray pill made from dried, ground animal thyroids. It contained both raw thyroid hormone as well as the converted form.

Within twenty-four hours of taking the first pill, all my old energy came roaring back as he had predicted. My heart was now healed, and I was once again healthy. He told me that the autoimmune disorder had probably been the cause of my heart attack but said I was now quite healthy and was probably going to live to a very old age, so I should get on with life.

I lost fifty pounds and let out my girly side. After living all those years as a lab rat, I swore to never wear jeans again.

It gets better! Years ago, in my early twenties, I could sing like a bird and was earning good money singing at embassies and a local bar in Washington, DC. I lost that singing voice shortly thereafter. The doctors told me that I had lesions (swollen, inflamed areas) growing on my vocal cords. They could not figure out the cause and, therefore, could not treat the problem. Bye-bye singing voice and singing career.

Instead, I completed my engineering degree and got a regular US Navy commission. They assigned me a designator of GURL (general unrestricted line officer), which is what they often assigned to female line officers. I proceeded to get married, see the world, and then resign my regular Navy commission. I came off active duty with a reserve commission so that I could have a family.

In my heart, I was still an arts and music person. I just did the engineering thing because it was the only way I could get the full scholarship I needed to go to college. With no singing voice, I just concentrated on instrumental music instead.

Back to the present. About a month after taking the first gray pill, I was walking around the house, humming a tune, as was my habit, when suddenly I realized I was singing! My singing voice was coming back! I melted in a flurry of tears of joy.

The doctor said the Hashimoto's disease had been the underlying reason I lost my singing voice, but now, as we managed the disease, the bad effects were going away.

I have been religious all my life, a lifelong Christian of the Episcopal branch of the "Jesus movement." My faith gave me the backbone I needed to endure the hard realities that life threw at me.

I was taught at an early age that sometimes God gives people great, unexpected presents. Unearned. Just right out of the blue. I was taught that when this happens, you respond in two ways.

First, you thank God continually (and really mean it).

Second, you tell other people about what happened (this is called witnessing). God gets a twofer (two for the price of one) out of this.

First, he has given his beloved child (and, according to my faith, every one of us is a beloved child of his) a wonderful gift. That gift reinforces and builds confidence in everyone who sees what happened in belief number one terms (God is good and loves giving good things to his children). Second, your witness testifies to the importance of belief number four (suicide is not a good answer).

Here's the bottom line: your witness gives people the hope they might need to carry them through adversity.

Since then, I've resumed my singing career.

Step by step, God has been leading me. One unlikely happening after another, I have been led to my current joyful situation. My first singing gig in fifty-five years was at a party I threw at my home for members of my development team after it was given a prestigious award by the Deputy Director of National Intelligence.

We jammed for eight hours after I introduced the young people present to jazz music from the repertoire of my youth. All present were shocked at what they heard. All they had known was this somewhat disabled scientist and program manager. They had never imagined I was capable of making such lovely sounds. Quite frankly, neither had I. I guess I had forgotten some important aspects of who I was. That was in June 2017.

Now I have sung in church choirs on both coasts and also joined an internationally acclaimed choral group, the Episcopal Chorale Society. We toured Ireland in March, 2018, and performed at Dublin's International Choral Festival.

We sang to a huge audience that filled St. Patrick's Cathedral, the largest church in Ireland. I sang first soprano. Twice we raised the roof, first when we sang gospel and second when we joined with three Irish choirs and the Orchestra of Ireland to sing several choral pieces from Handel's *Messiah*. The place exploded again as we sang the "Hallelujah" chorus. Talk about a fulfilling experience!

Now, I also sing with the Long Beach Camerata Singers, the Choral partner of the Long Beach Symphony Orchestra. Recently, 60 singers joined with 70 instrumentalists for a holiday special to an audience of over 3000 people at the Long Beach Convention Center. Again, as we performed Handel's Messiah, that audience also went wild when we sang the Hallelujah Chorus. What a personally-affirming experience to be part of something like that.

All this was totally unexpected six years ago. Then, I could never have imagined such a future, but it happened. Look at what I would have missed had I checked out with suicide at the height of my despair.

In summary, in relating this true experience I have addressed three of the four elements of the "walking with the Lord" core belief structure, as well as explicitly addressed number four: when given a choice, always choose life over death.

What about belief number three, love is our primary calling? While everything else I described above was taking place, another development was silently taking place. All my life, my faith taught me the importance of becoming the most loving person I could be. That doesn't happen by a person's own willpower but by human good intentions coupled with God's grace in the form of the guiding light of joy. Without me concentrating on that aspect of my life, I found something strange happening. Day by day, I was becoming more loving. I couldn't figure out why.

Finally, in prayer, the phrase "be ye perfect" kept popping into my head. I looked it up. The phrase is from Jesus's Sermon on the Mount, detailed in Matthew 5:48. In context, the original Greek word in that gospel is usually poorly translated in English as "perfect." A more accurate meaning is "completed" or "finished." I read further. It turns out that the notion of such "perfection" was a key concept taught by John Wesley, one of the founders of Methodism.

He explains it as being able to love others as God loves them. It doesn't mean being without human flaws or being sinless. In the context of Matthew's Gospel passage, it simply means loving like God. It is noteworthy that Jesus having said this implies that such perfection, in that sense, is attainable by humans. This is belief number three: love in our primary calling as human beings. God has been helping me blossom to be the person he created me to be, a loving child of a loving Father.

This last story hits all four beliefs. The value of the story is that every element I've described is verifiable by people who watched all this unfold.

Chapter Eight

SUMMARY

A major element of Jesus's life and ministry was devoted to teaching people by what he said and did so that they could turn their good intentions into effective action to make their lives more joyful, as well as assist in making this a better world. This was achieved by learning to discern the specific, personal will of the life force (which I, and many, call God) for them at each time and place of their existence. In other words, they sought to couple their actions in the material world to the guidance and assistance available to each human being from God.

This is what this book calls walking with the Lord.

Living life in this way transforms mere existence into a continuing joyful experience, even in the face of human tragedy. It also relieves people of the incredible burden of acting within their limited human capabilities while knowing that such actions can be inadequate and misdirected, likely to result in unintended harm to others, especially people they love.

The gospel song "Oh Happy Day" captures this perfectly with the phrase, "He [Jesus] teaches us to fight and pray and to live rejoicing every day."

This path of "living religion" extends and fulfills the usual religious practice of trying to follow a rigid set of rules put together at an earlier time, under different circumstances.

The importance of kenosis is asserted, the notion that God "emptied himself" of divine privilege in order to show suffering humanity how limited human beings (such as Jesus willingly became) could have joyful, fulfilled lives and play critical roles in carrying out God's saving action for the world.

A prerequisite for walking such a walk is to become mature in a core set of beliefs, based on the authority of personal observation and experience. In this way, the authority to act is the same authority exhibited by Jesus in his role as a limited human being like us. He showed us how to become one with God in a direct, personal way.

Without these beliefs being fully established, a person cannot walk with God in the way this book (and the Gospels) attest. These beliefs are as follows:

1. God is good - loving and gracious who wants only the best for us.

2. God communicates with us, and we learn to know our Master's voice and understand God's communications by a repetitive process of asking and receiving that we can call personal prayer.

3. Love is our primary calling as human beings, and God has endowed us with the potential to become perfected in our ability to love by following the joy that accompanies love given, received, and returned.

4. We must discipline ourselves to always choose life over death, living with as much joy as possible, whatever the circumstance. Only in this way can we avoid a permanent end that preempts any future possibilities of joy that we cannot foresee because of our limited human perspective and capabilities.

I recommend that groups of spiritually oriented people gather in the purpose of walking with the Lord for mutual support and learning. Take each element of the process as this book has described it and discuss events in your life experience that relate to that topic. Individually, take calculated bites of life in the Spirit and share the results, good or bad, with each other.

I have titled this book *Walking in Love,* which is the end result of walking with the Lord.

In this way, I think we will be doing what Jesus gave his life for as a witness and a teacher: "I come that they may have life, and have it more abundantly" (John: 10:10). Incidentally, the original Greek word (perisson) ordinarily translated as "abundantly" may be better understood as "beyond all expectations."

Maranatha! Come, Lord! Heal your children of this curse of unfulfilled, incomplete love.

As the presiding bishop of the Episcopal Church, Michael Curry, said recently in his address at the royal wedding of Prince Harry and Meghan Markle. Quoting the Reverend Dr. Martin Luther King, Jr., "We must discover love - the redemptive power of love".

Someone in the movies named Luke was able to do it, so we should be able. By his love, he saved his father. His last name wasn't Skywalker for no good reason.

Epilogue

A final commentary is in order. Reading this book takes the reader through the process of walking in love, but there are two more short subjects that need to be addressed. One deals with the beginning of the process and the other with the end, but both are interlinked.

Beginning-wise, a critical part of the process is for a person to be able to function adequately regarding prayer requests and answers to those prayers. That critical part is to listen to the divine through your "spiritual ears". This means you need to find and then cultivate the "place" in your consciousness where you can spiritually hear what the divine is communicating to you. In Jewish and Christian terms, this is what Psalm 46:10 refers to when it says, "Be still and know that I am God".

The most important aspect of being receptive to the divine relates to the modern mind, which has trouble being still. We are accustomed to a continual stream of distractions that captures our awareness and dilutes our ability to focus. In some cultures, this tendency is called "monkey brain", so-named for its similarity to the incessant chatter of monkeys. We must be able to screen out this stream of distraction if we are, spiritually, to hear what the divine is communicating to us.

The technique for strengthening our ability to focus is simple, and well-known across many cultures. In our Western culture it is called meditation. You train yourself to screen out the distractions by picking a phrase, a mantra. The phrase I used, which I learned in my youth from Eastern Orthodox "Hesychasts", is called the Jesus Prayer – "Lord Jesus Christ, Son of God, have mercy on me, a sinner". Incidentally, this name of the group I trained with comes from the Greek word "hesychia", which means "stillness".

Such a quest for stillness is at the core of the traditions of the contemplative order of monks at Mount Athos, in Greece. This doesn't mean you have to become a monk or nun to benefit from the practice. The tradition is very old, and exists in other cultures. For example, it also goes back many centuries to the Sanscrit mantra, "Om Mani Padme Hum – the jewel in the lotus". A beautiful teaching about it relates to the question, What does it mean?

The answer is, each of us is like a lotus blossom, a beautiful white flower blossom, that gradually unfolds its petals so that an observer can eventually see what is at the center of each blossom – a jewel. That jewel is you, the fully developed person the divinity created you to be.

To summarize the first point, then, a person needs to be able to still their "monkey brain" to effectively receive communications from the divine. To walk with God we need to sharpen up our ability to hear in a spiritual sense. In a Christian context, for example, Matthew 11:15 quotes Jesus teaching about this "One who has ears, let them hear". Incidentally, Jesus' teaching is based on his Jewish heritage. That teaching is found in the writings of the prophet Isaiah (Isaiah 32:3).

Why do we have this distraction problem, as humans? My answer is simple. Somewhere along the way, I think people developed the modern ego. It is this ego that makes us self-centered and rebellious. Rebellious about what? Rebellious about coming into a harmonious relationship with other people, with the rest of creation and with the divine.

We seem to have taken the gift of free will given to us by the divine and distorted it into an attitude that it is we, ignoring the very real limits of our human cunning and power, who think we are fit to run the world, instead of the divine. From this perspective, it is that ego that gives us "monkey brain" to block out our channel of relationship with the divine, our "ears". The arrogant ego feels threatened by the idea it is not in charge.

With this understanding, anger at God is misplaced, the idea that He, perversely, made us limited yet gave us rules for living a harmonious life that we cannot successfully carry out on our own. Instead, it is we who created the problem by our arrogant misuse of the gift of free will.

God didn't create the problem – we did. I think this is an important meaning behind the story of Adam and Eve in the book of Genesis. Once we had messed up the harmony of paradise by our own selfish arrogance, God gave us the cure – His beloved son, Jesus Christ. A Jesus who, emptied of divine privilege, by his life and teaching, showed us how an ordinary person could think and act, of their own free will, to restore a proper loving relationship with God, others, and the world – to lead us back towards paradise. This God is a loving, merciful God, not a perverse malicious one.

About The Author

Suzanne Miller is a versatile multitasker, having pursued careers in religion, science and engineering, and music, shifting from one to another whenever a major roadblock appeared and thwarted her progress. She's now retired from science and engineering and is putting her energies into singing and religious writing, now that modern medicine has given back her stamina (which she lost after a severe heart attack about sixteen years ago) and her singing voice (which she lost at the age of twenty-two).

Religiously, she is a former licensed lay vicar in the Episcopal Church, which has been her spiritual community for all of her adult life. Her original religious focus was pastoral care. She served for five years as the pastoral care assistant in a parish in Baltimore, Maryland, and later served in a similar role in a parish in Southern California. She also developed an adult education curriculum, which she used for many years in her various parishes.

She received her seminary training from the Claremont School of Theology and also studied church history and faith traditions in two separate live-in study sessions at St. George's College in Jerusalem.

After losing her singing voice, Suzanne shifted to a career as a naval officer, retiring as a commander in 1986. During a significant part of that time, she also worked in science and engineering (with a minor in religion). She served as an aerospace corporate scientist and executive, a senior civil servant in the Department of Defense., and finally (even though disabled) president of her own consulting company, where she led major new technical initiatives for the intelligence community. She was a member of that community for fifty-six years until she retired from defense work in March 2018.

Suzanne was enabled to pursue the previously noted secular work by early education in science and engineering. She holds a bachelor's degree in aeronautical engineering from the University of Virginia and a master's degree in engineering administration from the George Washington University. She completed all the coursework for a doctorate in applied mathematics at that same university before refocusing her attention, after twenty years of marriage, on her increased responsibilities as the newly divorced parent of her two boys.

She has had some notable health challenges in her life, most of which can be traced to an undiagnosed autoimmune disorder that had been the cause of her singing voice loss and finally resulted in a devastating heart attack a dozen or so years ago. That attack left her a semi-invalid (with severe loss of stamina) until advances in medical understanding and proper diagnosis restored her stamina and, surprisingly, her singing voice six years ago.

Freed of her health-imposed sedentary lifestyle, she lost fifty pounds, let out her girly side, and proceeds to joyfully participate in a less-restricted life.

Her energies are now focused on two of her previous career paths: singing and religion. Unlike her youthful career of singing for pay at embassy parties and a local bar in Washington, DC, her current singing activities are confined to singing for free in church choirs as well as membership in the internationally acclaimed Episcopal Chorale Society as well as the Long Beach Camerata Singers, performing both locally as well as internationally.

She has completed two singing albums. The first album is *It Ain't Over Till It's Over.* The second is *Walking In Love: Food For The Journey.* Both aim to put into song the messages of this book.

Her early investment in her own spiritual development (and significant on-the-job training in the hard-knocks of life) resulted in a robust religious faith that has been the bedrock that enabled her to endure all the hardships and career setbacks in her life. She never gives up hope and, as the gospel song "Oh Happy Day" says, she was taught to "watch, fight, and pray and live rejoicing every day."

In addition to this book, *Walking in Love: Why and How?* She published two earlier books, *Spirituality 101* and *Spirituality 202*, based on what she learned in her excellent seminary training.

She also recently has published another book: *I Am An American: Is America Racist?*, where she uses documented stories of individuals from her own family heritage to provide the reader with reliable, factual information they can use to address the important question contained in that last book title.